PAUL SHEFTEL   PHYLLIS LEHRER

I0140764

FOUNDATIONS
A Keyboard Musicianship Enrichment Program

PENTASCALES
INTERVALS
MAJOR SCALES
MINOR SCALES
CHORD CONSTRUCTION
CHORD PROGRESSIONS
RHYTHM AND NOTE DRILLS

YBK Publishers, New York

FOUNDATIONS: A Keyboard Musicianship Enrichment Program

Copyright © 2011 by Paul Sheftel and Phyllis Lehrer

YBK Publishers, Inc.
39 Crosby St.
New York, NY 10013

http://www.ybkpublishers.com

ISBN: 978-1-936411-04-7
Library of Congress Control Number: 2011925891

Manufactured in the United States of America
(or in England or Australia when for sale outside of the United States)

TABLE OF CONTENTS

PREFACE

Foundations derives from a larger project entitled *Personal Trainer*, a keyboard program offering musical workouts and enrichment activities for piano students of many ages and skill levels. Target areas include keyboard skills and technique (Explorations), sight playing (Eye-so-metrics), keyboard theory (Foundations) plus selected repertoire.

We felt that extracting the keyboard theory sections, *Foundations*, from *Personal Trainer* might serve the needs of certain players primarily interested in reinforcing their understanding of basic theory and, above all, in strengthening their knowledge of the piano keyboard. The keyboard can serve as an excellent map for helping to understand basic elements of theory. The term "keyboard geography" is often used in this regard. Relating keyboard patterns to theory is fundamental to relating the cognitive to the kinesthetic—the mind to the body.

Foundations covers:

- Five note major and minor scales (pentascales)
- Major and minor scales
- Intervals
- Chord construction
- Chord progressions
- Rhythm and note drills

Materials are presented sequentially. "Fitness Challenges" provide the player with carefully constructed drills that can serve the purpose of developing and increasing skills as well as for evaluating progress. Each challenge has a MIDI accompaniment specifically designed for that activity.

MIDI FILES

Each activity of *Foundations* has a carefully designed accompaniment in the form of a MIDI file. These accompaniments provide an invaluable enrichment to the entire program.

The MIDI files can be used interactively with a computer program called *Home Concert Xtreme* from Zenph Sound Innovations. *Home Concert Xtreme* displays the solo part in music notation and plays the accompaniment tracks in a musically coordinated fashion by following your tempo and dynamics. *Home Concert Xtreme* will even turn the pages for you!

For more information about obtaining the MIDI files please visit:
www.paulsheftel.com

To purchase *Home Concert Xtreme* or to download a completely free
demo version of the program, or to see a demonstration on video,
please visit: www.zenph.com

STUDY SUGGESTIONS

There is a great deal of material that is covered in *Foundations*. A study plan is offered on the following pages. This plan can serve for those wishing to work through the entire program. (The plan is incorporated into the five volumes of *Personal Trainer* also published by YBK Publishers.) The choice and sequence of materials should always be tailored to the specific needs of students and teachers. Some players may wish or need to focus on specific areas only, such as scales, chord progressions etc., and can fashion their own study plans accordingly. When players experience the application of concepts from *Foundations* to repertoire, these concepts come alive musically and are invaluable for the development of skills such as reading and memorizing. (In *Personal Trainer* every level has examples of repertoire deemed useful and appropriate to that level.)

It can safely be said that most books are designed to work in a linear fashion: you begin at the beginning and read or work through to the end. Foundations is not such a volume. Just as a balanced meal consists of items from different food groups, a balanced study program should include items from different groups. It would not be advisable for instance, to delay studying chords until every scale had been mastered. The study plan provided below is designed to emphasize a balanced approach to learning. It is strongly suggested that students work simultaneously on various selections from the different categories of scales, intervals and chords. It is also crucial that students incorporate a great deal of review and reinforcement into any study plan.

STUDY PLAN

Level 1
Pentascales
    all major *(Challenge #1—page 2)*

Intervals
    perfect 5ths *(Challenge #3—page 6)*
    major and minor 2nds and 3rds *(Challenge #3—page 6)*

Major Scales
    C, G D, A and E major—(one octave) *(Challenge #4—page 8)*

Chord construction
    major triads (root position) *(Challenges #7—page 16)*

Rhythms
    examples 1 – 3 *(page 31)*

Level 2
Pentascales
    major and minor *(Challenge #2—page 3)*

Intervals
    perfect 4ths *(Challenge #3—page 6)*
    major 6ths and 7ths *(Challenge #3—page 6)*

Scales
    C, G, D, A and E major two octaves *(Challenge #5—page 12)*
    a minor (three forms) *(Challenge #6—page 14)*

Chord construction
    triads: major/minor—root position *(Challenge #8—page 17)*
    triads: major, minor, dim., aug. *(Challenge #9—page 18)*

Rhythms
    Examples 4 – 5 *(page 32)*

Level 3
Scales
    F, B♭, E♭, A♭ major *(Challenge #5—page 12)*
    E, B and D minor (three forms) *(Challenge #6—page 14)*

Intervals
    minor 6ths and 7ths *(Challenge #3—page 6)*
    tritones *(Challenge #3—page 6)*

PENTASCALES

Before studying complete major and minor scales it can be useful to become comfortable playing 5-note scales, or "pentascales," in all keys. The major pentascale can be understood as a series of whole and half steps, the only half step occurring between steps 3 and 4. The C pentascale for example:

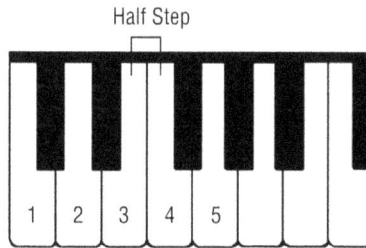

Any major pentascale, starting on any of the 12 keys, follows this pattern.

The 12 major pentascales can be reduced to 5 positions, or black/white color schemes

1. C and G (one color)
2. D/D♭ and A/A♭. (one black/white in the middle) Pentascales starting on black keys are always a color mirror of a neighboring white key. For instance:

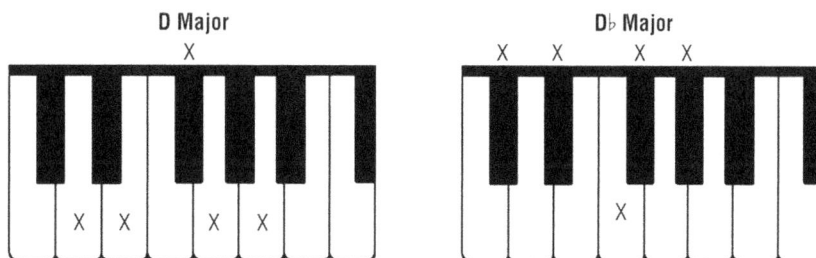

3. F (one black to the right)   F# (one white to the right)
4. E (2 blacks)   E♭ (2 whites)
5. B (3 blacks)   B♭ (3 whites

Practice the pentascale challenge outlined on the following page.

CHALLENGE #1

PENTASCALES — MAJOR

Proceed in the following order:

I ONE COLOR
C and G

II ONE BLACK/ONE WHITE (MIDDLE)
D and A   D♭ and A♭

III ONE BLACK/ONE WHITE (RIGHT SIDE)
F   F#

IV TWO BLACK/TWO WHITE
E   E♭

V THREE BLACK/THREE WHITE
B   B♭

CHECK LIST			
Starting Notes	**LH**	**RH**	**Both**
1. C and G			
2. D/D♭ and A/A♭			
3. F/F#			
4. E/E♭			
5. B/B♭			

CHALLENGE #2

PENTASCALES - MAJOR/MINOR

A major pentascale becomes minor by lowering the 3rd step. The half step now occurs between steps 2 and 3. Proceed through all these major to minor pentascales starting on the following notes and in the following order:

I   C and G

II   D and A   Db and Ab

III   F   F#

IV   E   Eb

V   B   Bb

CHECK LIST			
Starting Notes	**LH**	**RH**	**Both**
1. C and G			
2. D/Db and A/Ab			
3. F/F#			
4. E/Eb			
5. B/Bb			

INTERVALS

STUDY SUGGESTIONS

The following plan is offered for interval study:
1. 4ths and 5ths
2. Major intervals: 2nds, 3rds, 6ths and 7ths
3. Minor intervals: 2nds, 3rds, 6ths and 7ths
4. Tritones: augmented 4ths or diminished 5ths, depending upon spelling
   (C to F# = augmented 4th; C to G♭ = diminished 5th)

Some may find it helpful to locate white key/black key color combinations for finding intervals on the keyboard.

PERFECT INTERVALS

Perfect 5ths
- Always white/white except for the combination of B and F (B – F#)
- Always black/black except for the combination of B and F (B♭ - F)

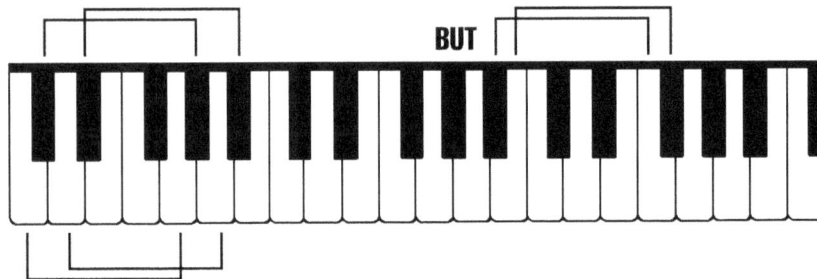

Perfect 4ths
- Mirror of perfect 5ths. Same color scheme.
  (ex. B to F# becomes F# to B; B♭ to F becomes F to B♭)

MAJOR INTERVALS

Major 2nds (whole steps)
- Always white/white or black/black except in gaps: E to F#; E♭ to F
                                                    B to C#; B♭ to C

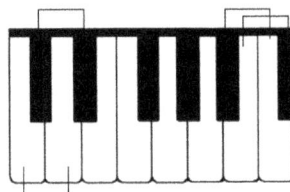

Major 3rds (identical to the order of major triads)
- Starting on C, F, G and G♭: white/white or black/black
- All others: white/black or black/white

Major 6ths
- Enlarge a perfect 5th by a whole step.

Major 7ths
- One half step smaller than an octave.
- Always white/black except for C and F
- Always black/white

MINOR INTERVALS

- "Major" intervals become "minor" when reduced by a half step.
- "Perfect" intervals become "diminished" when reduced by a half step
- Major and perfect intervals become "augmented" when enlarged by a half step
- A "tritone" consists of three whole steps and can be considered an augmented 4th or diminished 5th depending upon spelling.
  Example: C – F# = augmented 4th
                C – G♭ = diminished 5th

Minor 2nds (half steps)
- Always white/black or black/white except in the keyboard gaps: E to F, B to C.

Minor 3rds
- White keys starting on C, F, and G are white/black. All others are white/white.
- Black keys are black/white except for the gaps (i.e., E♭ – G♭)

Minor 6ths
- Enlarge a perfect 5th by a half step

Minor 7ths
- One whole step smaller than an octave or
- Always white/white or black/black except for 7ths starting on C or F (C to B♭; F to E♭).

Tritones
- Always white/black or black/white except for the combinations B–F and F–B

STUDY NOTE

This may seem like a great deal of information to learn and remember. It is! Master it all slowly and gradually—one interval at a time. Two examples are provided in Challenge #3. This scheme is to be used for every interval.

CHALLENGE #3
INTERVALS

Perfect 5th

Major 2nd

NOTE:
Use this scheme for all intervals.

CHECK LIST							
	LH	**RH**	**BOTH**		**LH**	**RH**	**BOTH**
Major 2nd				Perfect 5th			
Minor 2nd				Major 6th			
Major 3rd				Minor 6th			
Minor 3rd				Major 7th			
Perfect 4th				Minor 7th			
Tritone							

MAJOR SCALES
(ONE OCTAVE)

- By adding but three notes to a major pentascale we obtain the full major scale.
- The major scale can be understood as a series of whole and half steps, half steps occurring between scale degrees 3 – 4 and 7 – 8.

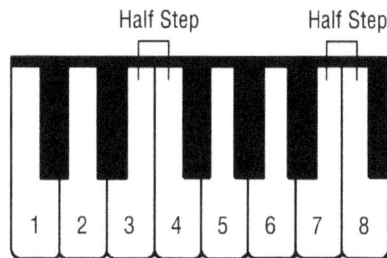

- Another way to conceptualize the major scale is by regarding it as two equally spaced groups of four notes (tetrachords) each having a half step between steps 3 – 4.

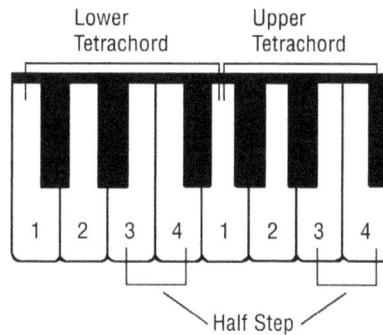

- Fingering for scales C, G, D, A and E (0 to 4 sharps) as illustrated in the major scale challenge:
  RH 4th finger on 7th step
  LH 4th finger on 2nd step

CHALLENGE #4

MAJOR SCALES - ONE OCTAVE

Transpose to G, D, A and E major.

CHECK LIST			
	LH	**RH**	**BOTH**
C			
G			
D			
A			
E			

MAJOR SCALES
(TWO OCTAVES)

While there are 12 major scales, there are only three fingering patterns. It is simply necessary to know where the 4th finger falls since it occurs but once in any octave.

Group I: 0 to 4 sharps (C, G, D, A and E)
> Fingering
>> RH: 4th finger on 7th step
>> LH: 4th finger on 2nd step

Group II: 1 to 4 flats (F, B♭, E♭ and A♭)
> Fingering
>> RH: 4th finger on B♭
>> LH: 4th finger on 4th step (except F, which is fingered like scales in Group I)

Group III: Enharmonic scales: B (C♭), F# (G♭) and C# (D♭)
> Fingering
>> RH: 4th finger on A# (B♭)
>> LH: 4th finger on F# (G♭)
> This is a very good group for two hand scale playing since the two hands work together with parallel fingering as shown in the examples on the following pages.

SCALE FINGERING TWO HANDS.

The three enharmonic scales, B, F#, and C# are known for being the most comfortable to play of all the major scales in that the long fingers are situated on black keys and, when playing both hands, the fingering is "parallel." The thumbs always come together on a white key (always in the gaps between the groups of black keys) and the black keys are played with the same fingering combinations (2-3/3-2 and 2-3-4/4-3-2).

The F scale also falls into this category even though the long fingers are not on black keys.

SOMETHING TO CONSIDER

The fingering suggested below is not traditional. However, there can be certain advantages to applying this fingering universally when playing scales with two hands: one fingering fits all and both hands are doing the same thing at the same time. The system is simple: thumbs are always together on the white keys in the gaps; fingers 2-3 are always situated in the area of the two black keys and fingers 2-3-4 in the area of the three black keys. Here are the examples in C and E major:

CHALLENGE #5

MAJOR SCALES - TWO OCTAVES
(Traditional Fingering)

CHECK LIST			
	LH	**RH**	**BOTH**
GROUP 1			
C			
G			
D			
A			
E			
GROUP 2			
F			
B♭			
E♭			
A♭			
GROUP 3			
B			
F#			
C#			

MINOR SCALES

The 12 minor scales can best be studied in the following groups:

1. a minor
   related to C major. No sharps or flats.

2. e, b, and d   G, D, F
   minor scales/white key tonics ⬌ relative major scales/white key tonics

3. g, c, and f   B♭, E♭, A♭
   minor scales/white key tonics ⬌ relative major scales/black key tonics

4. f#, c#, g#   A, E, B
   minor scales/black key tonics ⬌ relative major scales/white key tonics

5. d#, a#   F#, C#
   minor scales/black key tonics ⬌ relative major scales/black key tonics

MINOR SCALE FINGERING

All minor scales starting on white keys are fingered in the same way as their parallel major.

Starting on black keys there are a few exceptions:

Right hand: in the case of C# and F# minor, adjustments must be made for the harmonic forms. There are several options to explore.

Left hand: B♭ minor: 4th finger on 6th scale degree
           E♭ minor: 4th finger on 3rd scale degree

CHALLENGE #6

MINOR SCALES

There is a MIDI accompaniment for each of the 12 minor scales following the format shown above.

CHECK LIST							
	LH	**RH**	**BOTH**		**LH**	**RH**	**BOTH**
GROUP 1				**GROUP 3**			
A				F#			
E				C#			
B				G#			
D				**GROUP 4**			
GROUP 2				D#			
C				A#			
G							
F							

CHORD CONSTRUCTION

MAJOR TRIADS

A major triad consists of the 1st, 3rd, and 5th steps of a major scale.

KEYBOARD GEOGRAPHY

Major triads can be organized into three groups using the following color black/white color scheme:

1. C, F, G and G♭ all white/black
2. A, D, E and A♭, D♭ and E♭ (think "lemonade") one black/one white
3. B and B♭ (think ("killer B") two blacks/two whites

Many of the challenges in this section follow this scheme.

Notice that triads starting on black keys mirror neighboring triads starting on white keys.

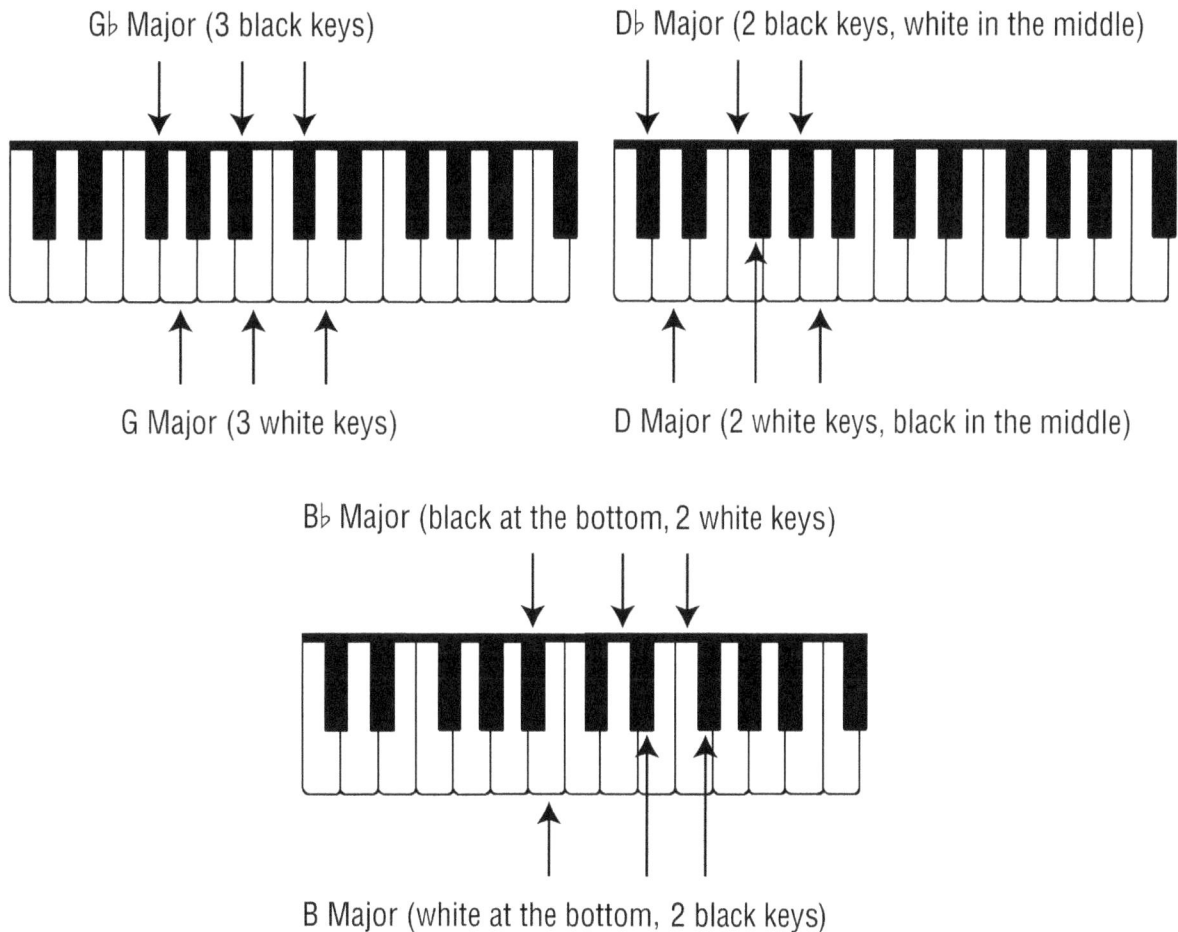

G♭ Major (3 black keys)

D♭ Major (2 black keys, white in the middle)

G Major (3 white keys)

D Major (2 white keys, black in the middle)

B♭ Major (black at the bottom, 2 white keys)

B Major (white at the bottom, 2 black keys)

CHALLENGE #7

MAJOR TRIADS - ROOT POSITION

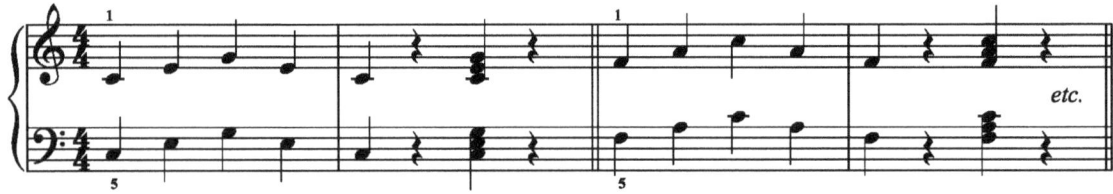

Continue through all keys in the following order (by color groups):

I   ONE COLOR
       C - F - G   G♭

II   1 BLACK/WHITE
       A – D - E   A♭ – D♭ – E♭

III   B   B♭

Use a variety of touches and dynamics.
Practice hands alone then together.

CHECK LIST											
	LH	**RH**	BOTH		**LH**	**RH**	BOTH		**LH**	**RH**	BOTH
GROUP 1				**GROUP 2**				**GROUP 3**			
C				A				B			
F				D				B♭			
G				E							
G♭				A♭							
				D♭							
				E♭							

CHALLENGE #8

MAJOR/MINOR TRIADS - ROOT POSITION

Continue through all keys in the following order using the following starting notes:

I	C - F - G	G♭
II	A - D - E	A♭ - D♭ - E♭
III	B	B♭

Use a variety of touches and dynamics.
Practice hands alone then together.

CHECK LIST												
	LH	**RH**	BOTH		**LH**	**RH**	BOTH		**LH**	**RH**	BOTH
GROUP 1				**GROUP 2**				**GROUP 3**			
C				A				B			
F				D				B♭			
G				E							
G♭				A♭							
				D♭							
				E♭							

CHALLENGE #9

TRIADS: MAJOR - MINOR- DIMINISHED - AUGMENTED

MAJOR | MINOR | MINOR | DIMINSHED | MAJOR | AUGMENTED

Continue ascending chromatically

CHECKLIST	LH	RH	BOTH
C			
C#			
D			
Eb			
E			
F			
F#			
G			
Ab			
A			
Bb			
B			

CHALLENGE #10

MAJOR TRIAD INVERSIONS

Continue through all keys in the following order (by color groups):

I   ONE COLOR
         C - F - G   G♭

II   1 BLACK/WHITE
         A – D - E   A♭ – D♭ – E♭

III   B   B♭

Practice hands alone then together.

CHECK LIST											
	LH	**RH**	BOTH		**LH**	**RH**	BOTH		**LH**	**RH**	BOTH
GROUP 1				**GROUP 2**				**GROUP 3**			
C				A				B			
F				D				B♭			
G				E							
G♭				A♭							
				D♭							
				E♭							

CHALLENGE #11

MAJOR/MINOR TRIADS FROM INVERSIONS

CHECK LIST											
	LH	**RH**	BOTH		**LH**	**RH**	BOTH		**LH**	**RH**	BOTH
GROUP 1				**GROUP 2**				**GROUP 3**			
C				A				B			
F				D				B♭			
G				E							
G♭				A♭							
				D♭							
				E♭							

CHALLENGE #12

INVERSION LOCATION

It is essential to be able to identify and locate a triad in an inversion without having to go back to the root position. The following challenge is designed for this purpose.

   1. Locate the root
   2. Find the interval of a 4th under the root
   3. Complete the chord

Work on one inversion at a time.

CHECK LIST											
	LH	**RH**	BOTH		**LH**	**RH**	BOTH		**LH**	**RH**	BOTH
GROUP 1				**GROUP 2**				**GROUP 3**			
C				A				B			
F				D				B♭			
G				E							
G♭				A♭							
				D♭							
				E♭							

CHALLENGE #13

BUILDING DOMINANT 7TH CHORDS

A dominant chord is built on the 5th scale degree of a major or minor scale (the dominant). This chord often has an added 7th

CHECK LIST											
	LH	**RH**	BOTH		**LH**	**RH**	BOTH		**LH**	**RH**	BOTH
GROUP 1				**GROUP 2**				**GROUP 3**			
C				A				B			
F				D				B♭			
G				E							
G♭				A♭							
				D♭							
				E♭							

CHALLENGE #14

BROKEN CHORDS IN EXTENDED POSITIONS

*or finger 3 on black keys

CHECK LIST											
	LH	**RH**	BOTH		**LH**	**RH**	BOTH		**LH**	**RH**	BOTH
GROUP 1				**GROUP 2**				**GROUP 3**			
C				A				B			
F				D				B♭			
G				E							
G♭				A♭							
				D♭							
				E♭							

CHORD PROGRESSIONS

PREFACE TO PROGRESSIONS

Harmonies can move from one to another in infinite varieties of ways but there are certain basic tendencies that are explored in the following progressions. Whether your ultimate goal is to play Bach and the classics, show tunes, rock or jazz improv, having a repertoire of basic progressions in your fingers will always be hugely useful.

HARMONY IN A NUTSHELL.

The closest relationships among chords occurs between the tonic and dominant, the triads (three note chords) that are built on the 1st and 5th degrees of the scale. The triad built on the 4th degree of the scale, the subdominant, is also closely related and moves easily to the tonic or dominant. These triads are called the primary chords of any key. In a major key, all three chords, I, IV and V are major.

Secondary chords occur on the 2nd, 3rd and 6th scale degrees. The chord built on the 2nd scale degree is called the Supertonic and it tends to move toward the V (Dominant) chord. The chord built on the 6th degree, or Sub-mediant, tends to move toward the Supertonic or ii chord, and finally the chord built on the 3rd scale degree, the Mediant (iii) tends to move towards the vi chord. The secondary chords in a major key are all minor. (Minor triads are usually indicated with lower case numerals.)

Simply stated, all chords, with the exception the subdominant, tend to resolve up a 4th (or down a 5th).

The following chord progressions illustrate these relationships and are presented in the following order:

I   The primary chords: .
      1. I - V – I
      2. I - IV – I
      3. I – V7 - I
      4. I - IV - V - V7 - I

II.   The Secondary chords:
      5. I - ii - V - V7 - I
      6. I - vi - ii - V7 - I
      7. I - iii - vi - ii - V7 - I

While fingerings are suggested, other fingering options can be explored.

The I - V - I progression is the fundamental progression in Western music. The progression is shown here from each of the three positions of the tonic chord. Practice each of these separately, hands alone, *in ascending chromatic order.*

CHALLENGE #15
I - V - I

CHALLENGE #16
I - IV - I

CHECK LIST FOR CHALLENGES 16 – 21					
	DATE		DATE		DATE
15.		18.		21.	
16.		19.			
17.		20.			

CHALLENGE #17

I - V7 - I

Remembering that the dominant chord often has an added 7th, the progression from tonic to dominant 7th is particularly simple. Both moving voices always move by half steps as illustrated in this challenge. (We are not including figured bass indications for inversions.)

CHALLENGE #18

I - IV - V - V7 - I

Continue the following, ascending chromatically through all the keys.

The following are to be played in the same manner, ascending chromatically. (The same MIDI accompaniment can serve for each example.

PROGRESSIONS USING SECONDARY CHORDS

Secondary chords tend to behave like dominants, resolving up a 4th (or down a 5th.) For instance, ii (lower case for minor chords) would tend to move to V (d minor to G major in the key of C). vi would tend to move to ii and thence to V (a minor to d minor to G major in the key of C). iii would move to vi etc. These tendencies are explored in the following challenges.

CHALLENGE #19

I - ii - V - V7 - I

Continue the following, ascending chromatically through all the keys.

The following are to be played in the same matter, ascending chromatically. (The same MIDI accompaniment can serve for each example.

CHALLENGE #20

I - vi - ii - V7 - I

Continue the following, ascending chromatically through all the keys.

The following are to be played in the same matter, ascending chromatically.
(The same MIDI accompaniment can serve for each example.

CHALLENGE #21

I - iii - vi - ii - V7 - I

Continue the following, ascending chromatically through all the keys.

The following are to be played in the same matter, ascending chromatically.
(The same MIDI accompaniment can serve for each example.

APPENDIX
RHYTHMS

The following rhythm challenges cover many of the most common rhythm combinations that players are likely to encounter in the earlier years of study.

Each of these challenges can be performed using *Home Concert Xtreme;* they can be tapped, clapped, or played on the keyboard using the key appropriate to the accompaniment in *Home Concert Xtreme.*

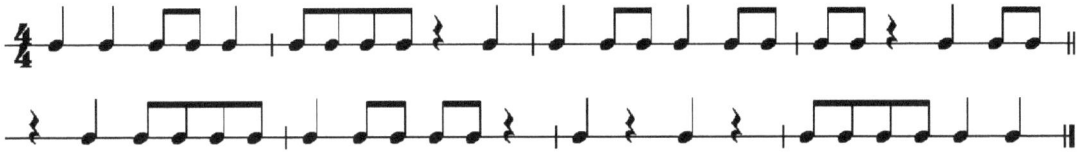

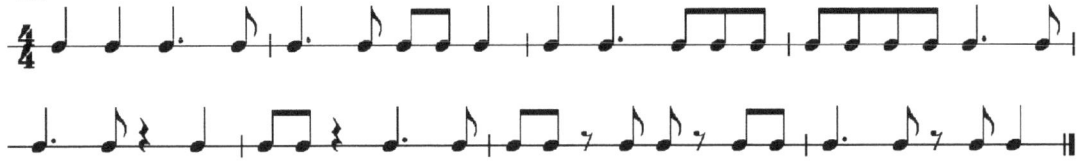

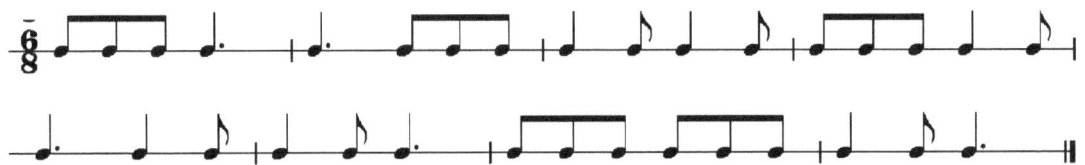

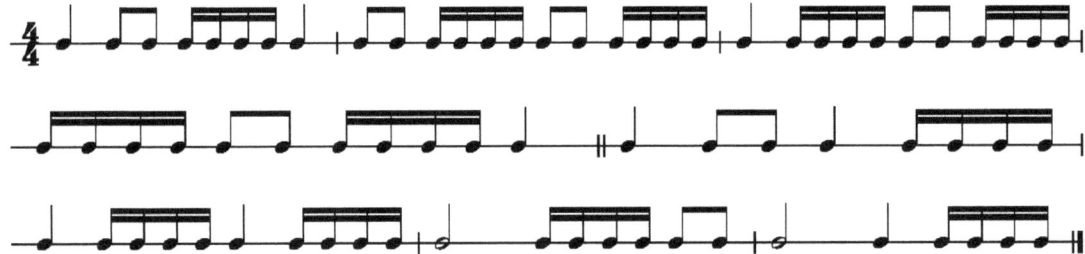

CHECKLIST	DATE
1.	
2.	
3.	
4.	
5.	
6.	
7.	
8.	
9.	
10.	

NOTE DRILLS

PREFACE TO NOTE DRILLS

Legend has it that there was, once upon a time, a piano teacher who claimed that she had her own unique style of teaching beginners, this was her claim:

The first week we go to notes and learn all the notes.
The second week we go to scales and learn all the scales
The third week we go to pieces.

We pretty much know now that we can't learn our notes and scales in so short a time.

In days of yore, and perhaps to this day, we, in all likelihood, would have been taught that the lines in the treble clef were best remembered as *E*very *G*ood *B*oy *D*oes *F*ine (or *D*eserves *F*udge). The bass clef was remembered as *G*ood *B*oys *D*o *F*ine *A*lways. The treble spaces were identified by spelling the word *F A C E* and the bass clef was *A*ll *C*ows *E*at *G*rass which, perhaps sometime after the industrial revolution, became *A*ll *C*ars *E*at *G*as

Identifying notes in this manner may have helped some, but for many it became a cumbersome crutch that, in turn, became a lifelong habit having the actual effect of slowing down reading. (And girls did not much like the "every good boy does fine" part— nor for that matter did the boys, who may not much have wished to do fine in the first place, soon discovering that there wasn't much truth to it anyway.)

It is now largely felt that, in general, identifying notes can be a mixed blessing for many students. Initially, certainly, it is of primary importance for students to recognize spatial relationships; up and down, steps and skips, musical patterns, etc., long before specific pitches are identified and recognized. Naming pitches can actually interfere with the reading process at this stage.

That said however, it soon becomes, at the least, necessary to be familiar with certain "landmark" or "guide" notes as these are often called. There are varied approaches. The one that we embrace is to start with middle, treble and bass Cs, as well as the treble clef G, and the bass clef F. We present these in Drill #1. The remaining drills focus on the following note groups:

High and low Cs; Gs and Fs.
Notes in the middle C area
Space notes
Line notes
Ledger line notes.

We have deliberately placed these drills at the end of Foundations to empha-size that note drills are an ongoing process. With time, note recognition, it is hoped, will become automatic through practice and one's exposure to much music. Other types of note drills (flash cards and the like) may play an ad-ditional small part in adding to the recognition process. We must recognize however that note recognition is but a small part of the total process of be-coming skilled in the challenging art of reading music.

CHECKLIST	DATE
1.	
2.	
3.	
4.	
5.	
6.	

NOTE DRILLS

Accompaniments are provided for each drill.

4.

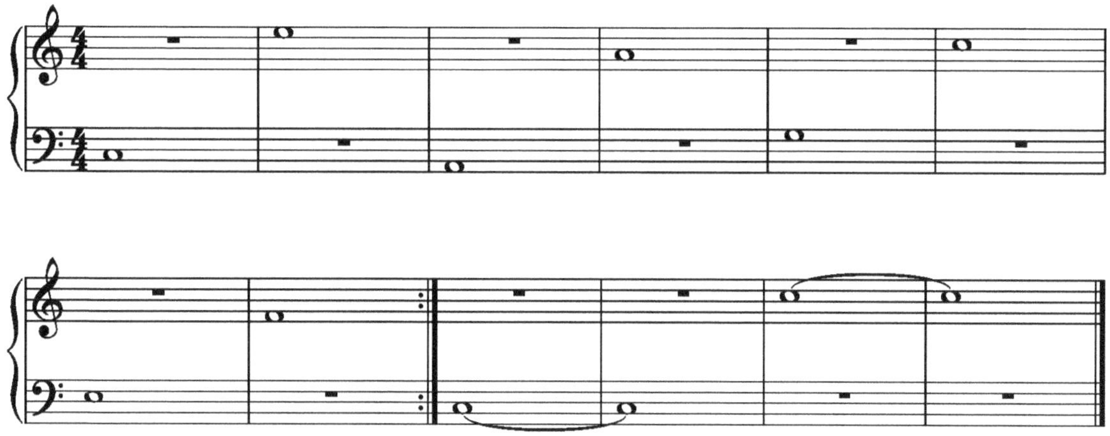

5.

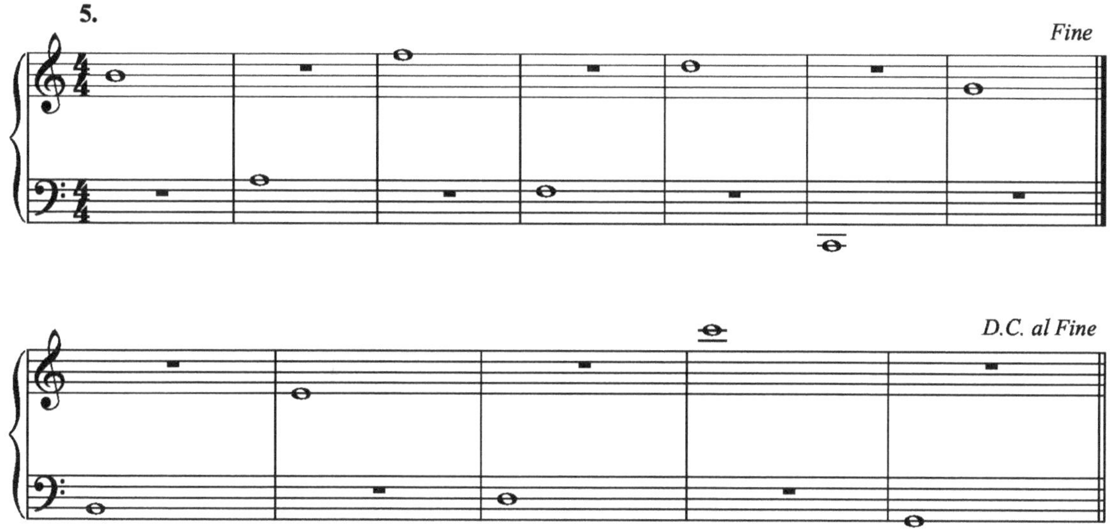

6.

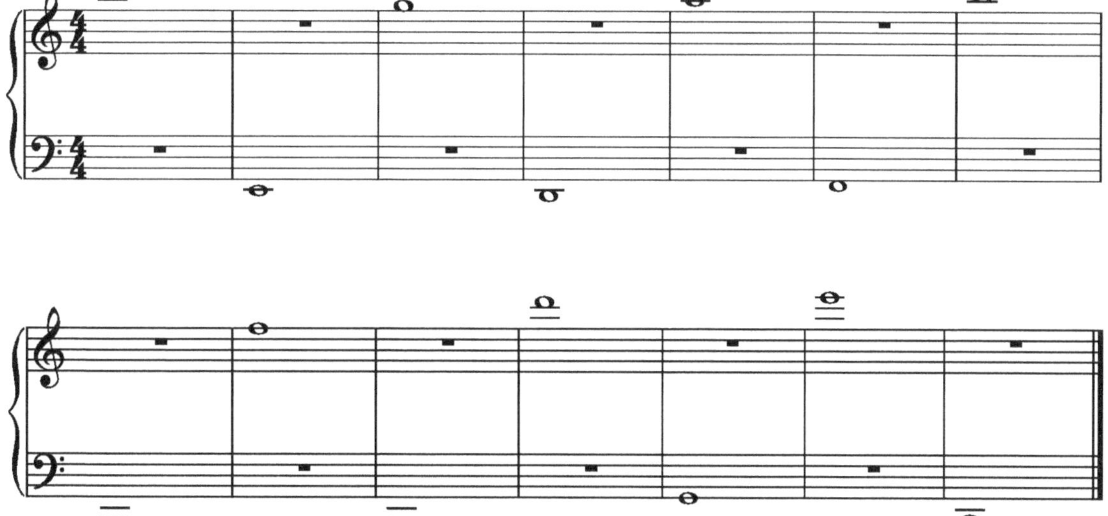

ABOUT THE
AUTHORS

PAUL SHEFTEL is a nationally recognized leader in the area of keyboard studies; his numerous published materials are widely used throughout the country. In his role as educator, he has performed, lectured, and conducted workshops in virtually every state in the United States. He has been a pioneer in the creation and development of instructional materials utilizing MIDI technology.

As part of the two-piano team of Rollino and Sheftel he performed throughout Europe and the United States, both in recitals and with such orchestras as the Berlin Philharmonic, the Royal Concertgebouw of Amsterdam, the Royal Philharmonic of London and the Chicago Symphony, among many others. He has appeared in two-piano and solo recitals in many of New York's leading concert halls, including Carnegie Hall, Town Hall, Alice Tully Hall, Merkin Hall, and Hunter College.

Mr. Sheftel is a graduate of the Juilliard School. His piano studies included work with Lazare Levy (in Paris), Edward Steuermann (at Juilliard) and Guido Agosti (in Rome on a Fulbright grant). Theory and composition: Mario Castelnuovo Tedesco and Alexander Tansman. In addition to his private teaching studio in New York City, he has served on the faculties of the Manhattan School of Music and Hunter College, has been piano editor for Carl Fischer, and is currently on the faculty of The Juilliard School where he teaches piano pedagogy.

PHYLLIS ALPERT LEHRER is known internationally as a performer, teacher, clinician, author, and adjudicator. She enjoys an active career as a soloist, collaborative artist, and clinician in the United States and such other coutries as Belgium, Canada, the United Kingdom, El Salvador, Taiwan, Japan, Sweden, Russia, Tajikistan, Brazil, and the Republic of Georgia. A founding member of the International Society for the Study of Tension in Performance, she contributes regularly to the Music Teachers National Association, the National Conference on Keyboard Pedagogy, and the World Piano Pedagogy Conference.

Ms. Lehrer's many articles, interviews, and reviews on piano pedagogy, music, and health have been published nationally and throughout the world. Her CD's include solos and duos with pianist Ena Bronstein Barton. In March of 2007 she was honored as a Music Teachers National Association Foundation Fellow, a program that "honors deserving individuals who have made significant contributions to the music world and the music teaching profession."

Ms. Lehrer has a Bachelor of Arts degree from the University of Rochester with music studies at the Eastman School of Music and a Master of Science in Piano from the Juilliard School of Music. Her teachers have included Paula Hondius, Lily Dumont, Adoph Baller, and Adele Marcus She is currently professor of piano and director of graduate piano pedagogy at Westminster Choir College of Rider University in Princeton, N.J.

www.ingramcontent.com/pod-product-compliance
Lightning Source LLC
Chambersburg PA
CBHW062109090426
42741CB00015B/3371